TUTANKHAMUN: TIME CAPSULE

By Mary Ann Johnson, Carol Oberling, and Betsy Rogers

Cartouche Publications
2220 - 126th Ave. Ct. E
Edgewood, WA 98372

The authors wish to express their gratitude to Kathy McMahon, Beverly Spalding, and Barbara Swenson for their contributions of specific ideas and activities; and to Shirley Tollefson for typing the manuscript.

Illustrations by Elizabeth Barlow

TUTANKHAMUN: TIME CAPSULE

A Personal Approach to the Treasures of

King Tutankhamun

What can the treasures of King Tutankhamun reveal about his life and the values of the Egyptian people who paid him honor as their leader and god? This book creates thinking activities surrounding the discovery of his tomb, his life and times, and how they compare with the life of a young person today.

This book stands alone with beautiful black design motifs from original Egyptian designs on his personal objects. It allows the reader to think personally about the meanings of these objects in comparison with today's values.

This material can be used with the user-friendly catalogue at the back of the book, or with pictures from many books and websites.

ESTABLISHING BEGINNINGS

Guessing about King Tutankhamun; includes chances to guess on general misconceptions about him and his tomb.

Learning some strange and amazing facts.

Exploring vocabulary by proposing and discovering meanings for mysterious, significant words.

Discovering the way the great event was announced.

Examining the mysteries and beauty of hieroglyphics (Cat. nos. 2, 7, 28, 33, 34).

DISCOVERING THE SCOPE

Dividing all objects in the Catalogue into categories (Cat. nos. 1 through 55).

Selecting, by a values clarification exercise, an object to purchase.

EXAMINING AND COMPARING OBJECTS

Comparing child's artifacts from Tutankhamun's tomb with artifacts of childhood saved today (Cat. nos. 1, 5, 8, 17, 41, and 46).

Comparing significance of ivory headrest with small casket containing balls of hair (Cat. nos. 48 and 9).

Comparing sculptures of King Tutankhamun as a boy and a man (Cat. nos. 17, 35, 38, and 41).

Discovering art principles portraying depth on flat surfaces (Cat. nos. 6 and 51).

Examining Tutankhamun's public and private images (Cat. nos. 13, 25, and 51).

Exploring the use of animals as symbols, then and now (Cat. nos. 4, 10, 11, 12, 16, 18, 23, 25, 32, 35, and 37).

CONSIDERING THE MUMMY, TOMB, AND AFTERLIFE

Discovering similarities between a trip on a prairie schooner and preparation for a journey to the afterlife (Cat. nos. 1 through 55).

Discovering the difficulty of preserving things.

Making a package to include present-day objects which reflect cultural values of our time (Cat. nos. 20, 21, 23, and 24).

CONTENTS

CONSIDERING THE MUMMY, TOMB, AND AFTERLIFE

GUESSING PAGE

T   F   1. King Tutankhamun was buried beneath a pyramid that was opened in 1922.

T   F   2. King Tutankhamun's tomb contained 55 objects, many made of gold.

T   F   3. King Tutankhamun ruled from age 21 to 39.

T   F   4. Some of Tutankhamun's necklaces were so heavy they had to be balanced with a decorated metal weight that hung down his back.

T   F   5. Some of the most important objects in King Tutankhamun's tomb were scrolls showing hieroglyphics.

T   F   6. Game boards and boomerangs were found in King Tutankhamun's tomb.

T   F   7. King Tutankhamun's mummy was found in a better state of preservation than that of most other mummies.

T   F   8. Many people objected to the removal of the mummy from the tomb.

T   F   9. King Tutankhamun's tomb was sealed so tightly that moisture could not get inside.

T   F   10. King Tutankhamun's wife and her belongings were also found buried in the tomb.

T F 11. Robbers stole over 100 gallons of precious oils from the tomb of King Tutankhamun.

T F 12. The boat in King Tutankhamun's tomb had to be a working replica of a navigable craft for him to be able to use it in his journey through the underworld.

T F 13. According to the Egyptian religion, only pharaohs and their families were allowed to be embalmed.

T F 14. The mummification process took seven days.

T F 15. It was considered sacrilegious to portray the pharaoh as a dog.

T F 16. No one was ever allowed to build anything over the sacred burial place of a pharaoh.

T F 17. After Carter's men dug down to the steps leading to Tutankhamun's tomb, Carter ordered the passageway covered, and waited over three weeks to explore further.

T F 18. Carter's discovery is even more surprising when one realizes he was looking for the burial place of another pharaoh when he accidentally came upon the tomb of King Tutankhamun.

T F 19. Besides much gold, the tomb held at least half a ton of silver objects of expert craftsmanship.

T F 20. The mummy was found wrapped in three layers of pure linen.

Answers to these questions are on pages 97 and 98.

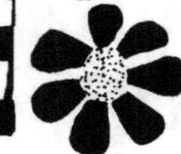

TWELVE STRANGE AND AMAZING FACTS

ABOUT KING TUTANKHAMUN AND HIS TREASURES

1. King Tutankhamun's mummy was one of about 731 million mummies that were prepared for burial in Egypt over a period of about 4,500 years.

2. King Tutankhamun's mummy was wrapped in many layers of linen bandages. This same kind of linen became very much in demand during the 19th Century. Because of a shortage of rags for making paper, Egyptian mummies were stripped of their bandages, and the bandages sent to America where they were converted into brown wrapping paper.

3. The mummies of two unborn babies were found in King Tutankhamun's tomb. These may have been two children of the king and queen, or they may have been the unborn babies of other people. It is thought they were placed in the tomb to symbolize the wish for the rebirth of the king.

4. In some instances, perfumed oils made of animal fat and resins, were considered to be even more valuable than gold. Two robberies occurred before the tomb was finally sealed. In the second robbery, what amounted to 105 gallons of precious oils were taken, and many items of gold were left behind.

5. Many white oval wooden containers which were found in the tomb were similar to present-day cans of meat. These contained mummified parts of ducks and mutton, all meant to be eaten by King Tutankhamun in the afterlife.

6. Some dead insects and spiders were found in the tomb. These were compared with the same species found in Egypt today. It was discovered they have not changed at all in over 3,000 years.

7. Only a few objects of silver were found in King Tutankhamun's tomb. See Catalogue number 50 for one of these, a pomegranate vase. Ancient Egypt used much gold, but very little silver.

8. During King Tutankhamun's reign, elaborate feasts were held at which the guests were given collars of fresh flowers. Also, small cakes of perfumed oil were placed on the guests' heads. As the oil melted, it added scent and shine to their wigs.

9. King Tutankhamun's mummy was the only mummy which was found buried in three caskets. The two outer ones were made of wood overlaid with beaten gold, but the innermost casket was made of solid 22-carat gold. It weighed 296 pounds.

10. One of Howard Carter's helpers, James Henry Breasted, worked alone in the tomb copying and deciphering the writings on the walls. While working, he heard rustling and whispering sounds all around him. At first afraid, he finally reasoned that these sounds were creaks and groans coming from wooden objects in the tomb. After having been closed up for over 3,200 years, they were adjusting to the changing temperature and humidity.

11. Later, in the dim light of the tomb, Breasted thought he saw the eyes of two of the statues move. He found that this illusion was created when tiny particles of mica fell from the eyes of the statues. These particles caught the light of Breasted's flashlight and made the eyes seem to move.

12. Historians do not consider King Tutankhamun to be a great pharaoh. But he has received more attention than all of the other pharaohs, because his was the first tomb to be discovered containing an undisturbed royal mummy and its treasures.

STRANGE-SOUNDING WORDS

New and strange sounding words are often encountered when an unfamiliar period of history is investigated. By yielding to their novel sounds and enjoying their unfamiliar configurations, a person can acquire a sensitivity for the depth and beauty of the language of that historical period. The English words which are derived by translating hieroglyphics from the tomb of King Tutankhamun are often very strange to see or hear. Some are written for you below. If you would like to unravel their meanings, it might be fun to do so by participating in a word game. Directions for the game follow the list of words:

canopic	fellahin
corporeal	viscera
unguent	burnisher
cartouche	lunar
sarcophagus	pectoral
necropolis	scarab
pillage	amulet
scepter	kohl
ibex	henna
mastaba	scimitar
millennium	counterpoise

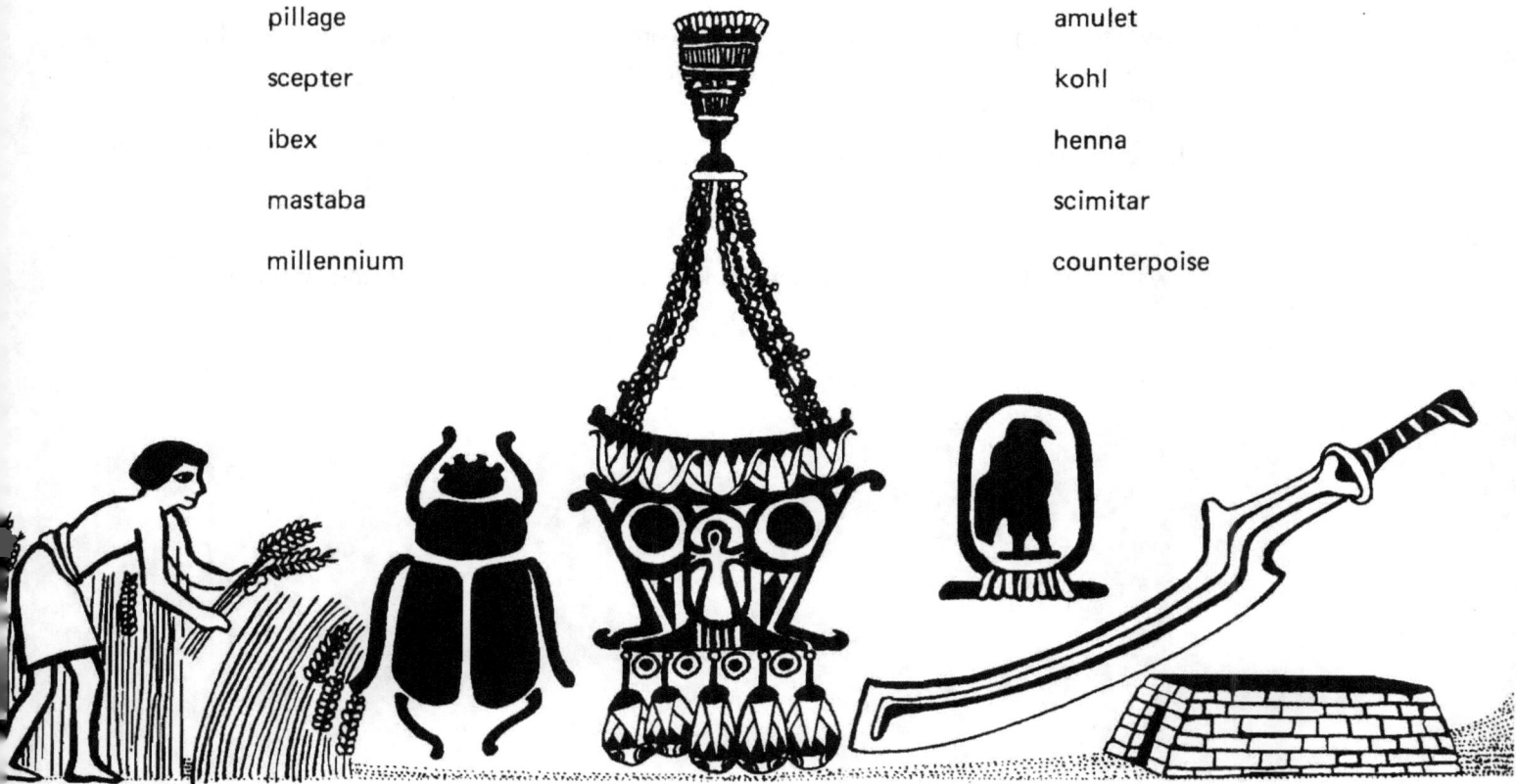

You will need a small stack of one inch by four inch strips of paper and a dictionary.

1. First, cross out any words which are familiar to anyone in the group.

2. Appoint an outsider, or group leader, to print out a brief dictionary definition of each word on one of the four inch strips of paper.

3. Taking the words one at a time, have each group member write a guessed definition on a strip of paper and give it to the leader.

4. Have the leader hide the real definition among the guesses, and read all definitions to the group.

5. Let each group member guess which is the real definition.

The winner is the person guessing the most actual definitions for the words used in the game.

IMPORTANT MESSAGES

You are Howard Carter, it is the fall of 1922, and you are getting desperate. Consider these facts:

1. You are the only archeologist who is digging for treasure in The Valley of the Kings, since only one license, or concession, is granted per year to someone to dig in the area.

2. You have already been searching for King Tutankhamun's tomb for eight years. You have only about two months left, from the end of October until mid-December, to do your excavating for treasure; the heat is too great and the winds too fierce prior to the month of October; tours of the area at Christmastime must not be interrupted by your work.

3. You have been told by your rich sponsor, Lord Carnarvon, that he is unwilling to finance any further searches since he has already lost much money in fruit-less searches (over $500,000 by present standards.) If you are again unsuccessful, you have guaranteed him that this last venture will be reimbursed by you.

4. You have dug almost everywhere in the area where pharaohs were buried, except in an area where workmen built huts when working on the tomb of another pharaoh, Ramesses VI. The area is now heaped with rubble. Two years ago you gave up digging in this area, thinking it unlikely that huts would be built over an area saved for the burial of a pharaoh.

5. Your project rests upon the shoulders of fifty men and boys who will put the tons of rubble into baskets and carry it away from the lower valley burial area. They will dump the contents on higher ground, and return the empty baskets to be refilled.

6. Most people believe the area has been picked clean, since the tombs of thirty-three pharaohs have been discovered prior to this time. Every one of these tombs had been invaded by robbers who had virtually stripped the tombs of their objects of value.

7. Only a few objects bearing the strange name of Tutankhamun have been found. They could be indicators of a burial very nearby, or they may not.

As you arrive at the site of the dig on the morning of November 4, 1922, you are aware that no one is working. The silence is significant. Workmen have discontinued their efforts because they have come upon a stairway located under the first hut which they have removed. They are waiting for you.

You quietly direct the men to dig down and uncover the staircase. Step by step, your discovery is affirmed. The top of a doorway comes into view. You are stunned to see that the doorway is still sealed.

Now, speculate: What are the first three things you will need to do?

1.

2.

3.

If you wish to compare your choices with those of Howard Carter, here is what he did:

1. He ordered the stairway refilled.
2. He ordered the stairway heavily guarded.
3. He sent a telegram to his sponsor, Lord Carnarvon, back in England.

The words of that telegram have become a famous example of unselfishness and restraint. Altogether, he used twenty words to announce the exciting news to his friend and patron.

Consider what you would say if you were allowed between twenty and twenty-five words to share the information Howard Carter cabled to his friend. A telegram form is provided for your message.

Share what you have written with a small group, and see what others have written. Either select the one you think is best, or combine your best work to create one message. Compare your result with the work of other groups.

Now, read the actual message that Howard Carter sent to his friend on the morning of November 6, 1922:

AT LAST HAVE MADE WONDERFUL DISCOVERY IN VALLEY:

A MAGNIFICENT TOMB WITH SEALS INTACT: RE-COVERED

SAME FOR YOUR ARRIVAL: CONGRATULATIONS.

Compare that message with the one you composed:

1. Which had more information?

2. Which was more exciting to read?

3. Which showed more modesty?

4. Which one do you think would appeal the most to Lord Carnarvon?

5. Which has the better wording to record an historical event?

HIEROGLYPHICS

Until 1799 all we knew about hieroglyphics was that they were pictures with hidden meanings. In that year French soldiers who were digging trenches for one of Napoleon's battles in Egypt discovered a broken slab of rock with strange markings on it, much like the one above. Since it was found near a place called Rosetta, it became known as the Rosetta Stone.

In the illustration above, the two enlarged areas show the name of Ptolemy, which Champollion discovered written in Greek and in hieroglyphs.

The Rosetta Stone was composed of three bands. The top band showed hieroglyphics, the middle band showed a more simplified Egyptian writing, and the lower band showed a message in Greek. It took the genius of a Frenchman, named Jean Francois Champollion, to discover the meaning of one word of hieroglyphics. He did this by linking it with one Greek word on the third band. His breakthrough came after 14 years of study from a copy of the writings on the stone. He operated from an idea that almost everyone else had overlooked — that the pictures represented sounds which spelled words.

Most people had tried to decipher the hieroglyphs as direct pictures of words; for instance, that a picture of a bird meant **bird.** Much of the time, however, the combinations of pictures did not seem to make any sense.

The one word which held the key of discovery for Champollion was the name **Ptolemaios** (Ptolemy). He was a Greek general who invaded Egypt and was so powerful, he started a new line of pharaohs. Champollion noticed that a cartouche containing the name of a pharaoh appeared the same number of times in hieroglyphics as the name of Ptolemy appeared in Greek. He guessed that the cartouche also contained the name of Ptolemy. This proved to be correct.

Later that year Champollion was able to perceive more about the nature of hieroglyphics. He found that the messages in cartouches facing three different directions were identical. They all contained the name of the pharaoh, Ptolemy.

Study the three cartouches below, which contain the name of Tutankhamun. What discoveries about hieroglyphics can you make by comparing these three ways of writing his name?

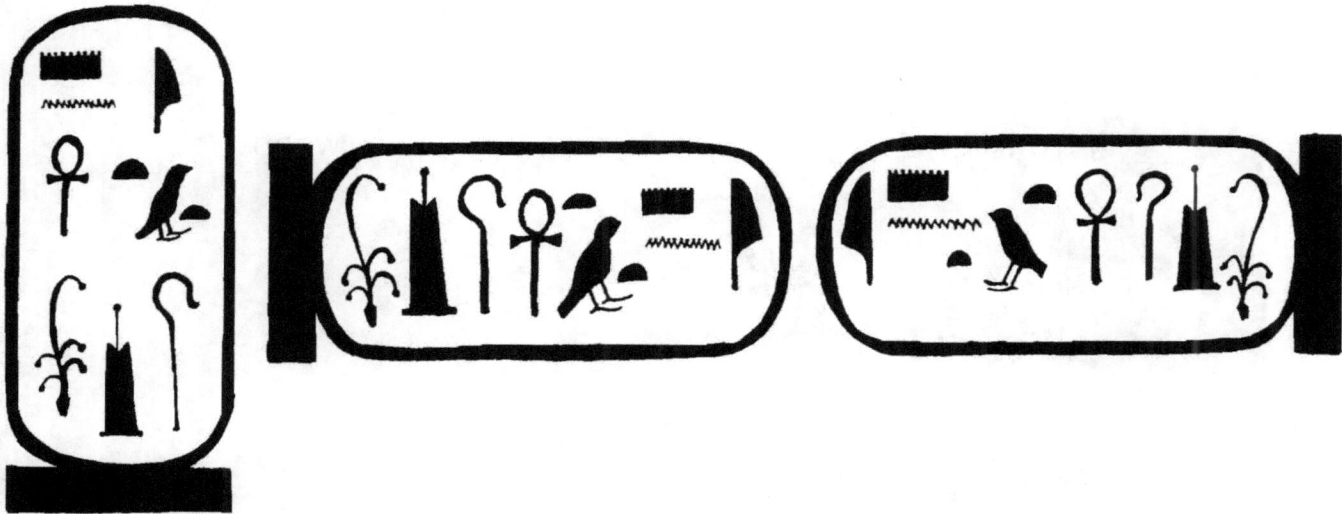

CLUES	DRAW YOUR CONCLUSIONS
1. What hieroglyphs show the end of Tutankhamun's name? Note the stands of the cartouches.	1.
2. If you know that the animal hieroglyphs always faced the first hieroglyph in the message, can you draw the first hieroglyph in Tutankhamun's name?	2.

15

Eventually it was discovered that twenty-four of the pictures in hieroglyphics stood for consonant sounds, approximately like the sounds of our letters **r**, **m**, and **s**, for instance. Many other pictures stood for sounds that were more complex. No sounds corresponding to our vowels seemed to have been used. About one hundred of the pictures used in hieroglyphics, did, in fact, stand for the ideas they actually showed.

To see how some of our words would look if they were written in a picture code, some English words are pictured in the chart below. See if you can decipher how the words would be written in the English alphabet:

PICTURE CODE — ENGLISH WORD

1. 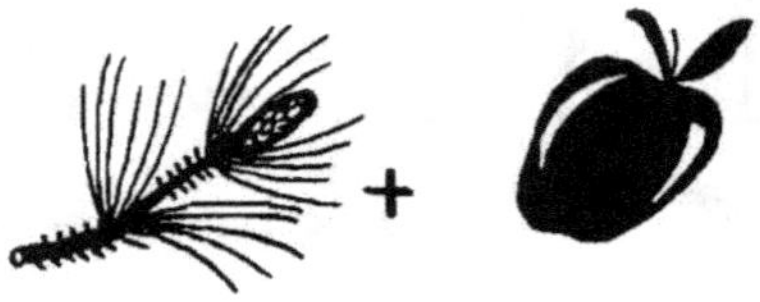 1.

2. 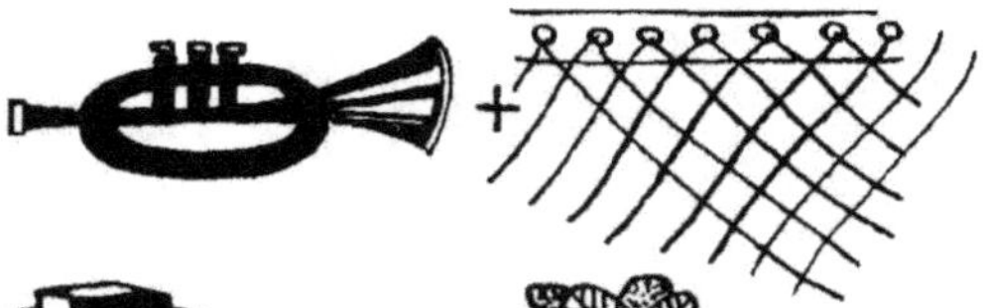 2.

3. 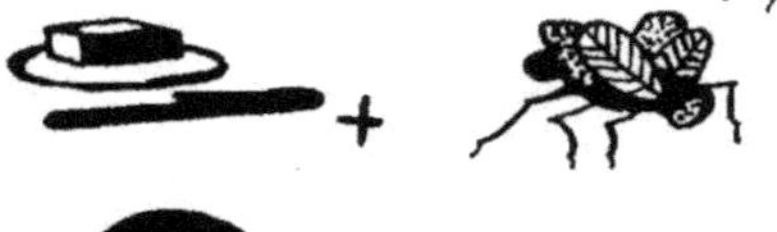 3.

4.  4.

5.  5.

When a word is shown in pictures to convey the sounds of its syllables, we call the pictures a **rebus**.
What pictures can you create to make a rebus for the following words:

ENGLISH WORD	PICTURE WORD (REBUS)
1. potluck	
2. mountaineers	
3. rocking	
4. honeymoon	
5. frisbee	

Can you think of two other words to represent in picture form?

ENGLISH WORD	PICTURE WORD
1.	1.
2.	2.

Now that you have tried writing some words using pictures as sounds, you may be able to understand why this language was so difficult, both to write and to decipher.

When King Tutankhamun ruled Egypt, most people did not know how to write hieroglyphics. Hieroglyphs were most often carved in stone or drawn on sheets of papyrus. The burnisher, used for polishing paper (Cat. no. 34) and the pen holder (Cat. no. 33), which were buried with King Tutankhamun, were probably never used by him in his lifetime, but were included for use by one of the gods in the afterlife.

In Egyptian society the scribes were the only people who knew how to write. They were so important that they were not required to do physical labor nor to pay taxes.

Since the written language of your culture is taught to almost everyone, even as a young child, certain qualities of that language differ from the complicated language of hieroglyphics.

Consider these differences:

QUESTIONS	YOUR LANGUAGE	HIEROGLYPHICS
1. Which one is the easier and faster to write?		
2. Which one is more beautiful in shape and form?		
3. Which one has the clearer meaning?		
4. Which one is more fun to work with?		
5. Which could be used more easily for design and decoration?		

To compare your language and hieroglyphics, you would also have to know some of the following facts about hieroglyphics.

1. You have already discovered that animals in a hieroglyph always faced toward the beginning of the message, and all of the animals in one message faced in the same direction. Hieroglyphs were read from left to right, or from right to left, depending upon which way the animal symbols faced.

2. The most important hieroglyphs forming a royal name were placed first in the set of hieroglyphs. Thus ▮ came first in Tutankhamun's name because it was the most important symbol in the hieroglyph for his name.

3. Hieroglyphs contained no punctuation.

4. The scribes of ancient Egypt used to write the names of their pharaohs inside an oval ring representing a length of rope with the ends tied together. French scholars later named these oval rings **cartouches.**

5. Sometimes the cartouches were used without a message. The encircled space was then meant to suggest that all the space contained in the universe belonged to the pharaoh.

6. Number ideas were also conveyed by picture symbols in hieroglyphics. For instance, a palm rib represented a year; and a tadpole represented the number 100,000.

Hieroglyphs were so beautiful that they often were used as decoration, as well as to convey a message.

In comparison, very little use is made of our language for decorative purposes. Can you think of any objects in your home in which our language is used for decoration?

1.

2.

3.

What are your opinions about your language as compared with hieroglyphics? Fill in the blanks below.

ALPHABET	
Advantages	
Disadvantages	

HIEROGLYPHICS	
Advantages	
Disadvantages	

PUTTING THINGS INTO GROUPS

There were over 5,000 objects in the tomb of King Tutankhamun. Fifty-five of them were on tour in the United States during 1976 — 79 to celebrate the 55th anniversary of the discovery of King Tutankhamun's tomb. These objects are listed for you on the following pages. In addition, you will find a picture and full description of each object in the Catalogue at the back of this book.

Your job is to arrange the objects on this list in some interesting ways. Make everything fit into five groups, or more. Look closely at each object, and read the brief description of it in the Catalogue.

Before you start, think about some of the ways you can put things into groups. Some examples are:

1. By their shape

2. By their use or purpose

3. By their value (historical value, money value, beauty).

Remember: You need to organize the objects into at least five categories.

THE FIFTY-FIVE OBJECTS

1. Painted wooden head of King Tutankhamun
2. White alabaster cup
3. Trumpet and wooden stopper
4. Carved leopard's head
5. Crook and flail (rod and staff)
6. Belt buckle
7. Portable chest
8. Child's chair
9. Miniature alabaster casket
10. White alabaster vase for oils
11. Folding stool
12. Chair from coronation
13. Gold-plated shrine, or case, for a goddess
14. Alabaster lamp resembling three lotus blossoms
15. Carving of a headless animal, hung from a pole
16. Jar for oils, with resting lion on lid
17. Small gold staff
18. Ostrich-feather fan
19. Lidded case for oils, with double cartouche design
20. Golden dagger and sheath
21. Bead bracelet
22. Gold rings
23. Flexible collar in the form of a vulture
24. Necklace with vulture pendant
25. Gold mask found over head and shoulders of the mummy
26. Gold pectoral with emblems of the sun and moon
       (ornament worn over the chest)
27. Falcon pectoral
28. Cartouche-shaped box

29. Gold earrings
30. Mirror case
31. Necklace with moon emblem and lotus counterpoise
32. Scarab beetle bracelet
33. Pen holder
34. Papyrus burnisher: paper polisher
35. Statue of King Tutankhamun with harpoon
36. Model boat
37. Golden statue representing a cobra as a god
38. Statue of King Tutankhamun riding on a leopard
39. Golden statue of a god, Ptah
40. Carved mummy of Tutankhamun lying in state
41. Squatting solid gold figure of a king
42. Wooden carving of King Tutankhamun
43. Wooden figure of the goddess, Selket, overlaid with gold
44. Alabaster stopper for canopic chest, resembling head of
       Tutankhamun
45. Miniature coffin for one of the king's internal organs
46. Double-sided game board
47. Flask of alabaster
48. Headrest
49. Model of a folding stool
50. Vase shaped like a pomegranate
51. Wooden clothing chest with carvings of the king and queen
52. Royal scepter with elaborate gold designs
53. Jar for oils, shaped like standing lion
54. Jar for oils, resembling resting ibex, or deer
55. Decorated bow

TREASURES TOURNAMENT

You and seven of your advisors, all highly respected art patrons, are recognized for your knowledge of the treasures of King Tutankhamun.

Because of your expertise, you have been asked by a group of artists to nominate the one object, from the fifty-five on tour in the United States, which you think would be the most valuable to purchase. Other groups from other areas of the country will be making similar nominations.

A panel of distinguished American artists will consider all the objects nominated, and will choose the most prized object for purchase. The designation of this panel of three experts should be made before proceeding, as this group will not participate in the nomination process.

Discuss and compare the categories you have already created on pages 23 and 24. Then list the four categories your group decides are the most important:

1.   3.

2.   4.

Use the following steps to complete the Treasures Tournament Selection Form on page 28:

1. Look back at all of the objects in each of the four categories you have selected. Pick the two objects in each category which you think are the most important and appealing. Fill them in on the Selection Form, in the blanks marked **Quarter Finals.**

2. Each of you will now perform the difficult task of selecting only one of the two objects listed. Present an argument to the rest of the group telling why you think it is the one object that would be the best to recommend for purchase.

3. After all of you have presented your arguments, narrow down the list by picking the better object from each category. Write the names of the winning four objects on the Selection Form in the blanks marked **Semi-Finals.**

4. For the next round, your task is a bit harder. Two objects from different categories must be compared. Team up with a partner to present an argument for one of the objects which has been selected in the Semi-Finals. A vote on these four must then be made to select the one you will write in the blanks marked **Finals.**

5. For the Finals, only two objects will be compared. Every member of the group must give one reason for purchase and one reason against purchase of each object.

6. Your group must then make its final vote to select the one object you will recommend for purchase. Write this in on the Selection Form as your Winner.

When you have finished this work, you will submit your choice to the panel of distinguished American artists so it can be compared with the winners of other nominating groups. You may need to defend your choice before the panel. So that you will be well prepared for this task, write a list of the arguments your group would use to defend the object you have chosen to recommend for purchase:

1.

2.

3.

4.

The panel of noted artists must now choose and state reasons for its choice:

DECISION: _____

Reasons: 1.

2.

3.

4.

You deserve great credit if you can boast that your nomination was the final choice. In any case, your choice has impressive merits which you have intelligently portrayed.

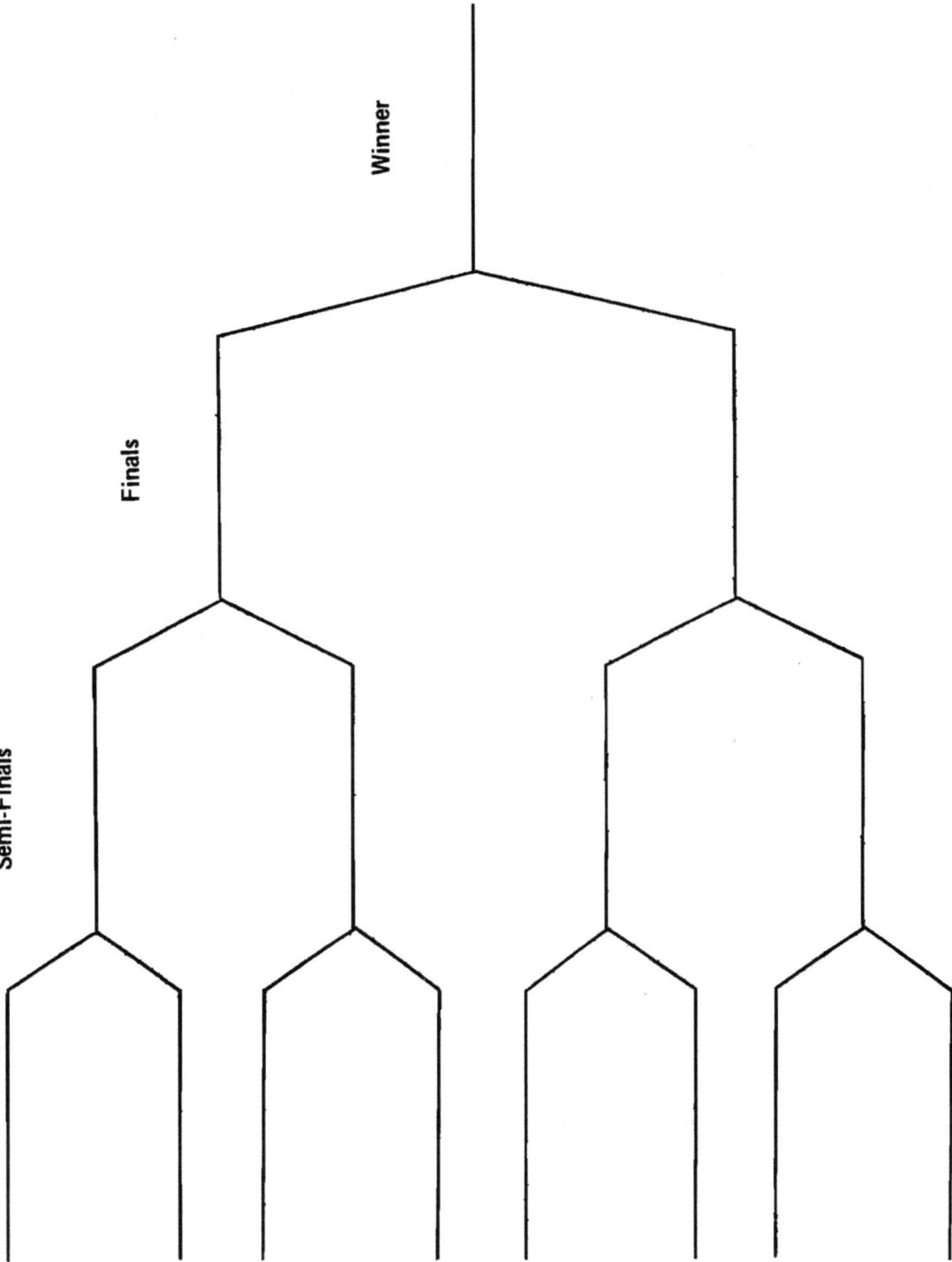

SELECTION FORM

Quarter Finals

Semi-Finals

Finals

Winner

CHILD'S TIME CAPSULE

Throughout history, people have enjoyed seeing the things that have been saved from their childhood. From parents, grandparents, and others, they have learned interesting details of their early years of life.

Before viewing the objects portraying the birth of King Tutankhamun, consider the event of your own birth. Can you remember some things you have been told about it?

1. What day of the week were you born?

2. What time of day were you born?

3. Were you born in a hospital?

4. Were you bald?

5. Were you noisy or quiet?

Catalogue number 1, pictured below, represents the moment of birth of the infant sun god, Ra. His head is shown coming out of a lotus blossom. The features seem to be those of Tutankhamun. It is believed that having this model in his tomb allowed King Tutankhamun, by some magical process, to be reborn each day as the sun god.

1. What is "wrong" with this statue, if it really was meant to represent King Tutankhamun as a newborn baby? For example, notice the ear lobes.

2. Was he bald?

3. Was he noisy or quiet?

Several objects from childhood were found in King Tutankhamun's tomb. Since he became a pharaoh near the age of nine years, he was the owner of ceremonial as well as personal objects during his early years of life. Some of these have been included in the treasures on tour. Write in the name of the object; then write what you think the object shows about the early years of Tutankhamun's life.

Catalogue number	Object	What does it show about the childhood of Tutankhamun?
1		
5		
8		
17		
41		
46		

With a partner or small group, list what objects are most commonly saved from childhood by people today. Together decide on six of the objects you think would best show what childhood is like today.

POSSIBILITIES	OBJECT	WHAT DOES IT SHOW ABOUT THE CHILD OF TODAY?
_____		
_____		
_____		
_____		
_____		
_____		
_____		
_____		
_____		
_____		
_____		
_____		

Final discussion:

1. Listen to the choices of other people. Now that you've heard them, would you want to change any items on your list?

2. Were any items on the present day list similar to the items of King Tutankhamun?

HEADREST AND HAIR BALLS

Some of the objects in King Tutankhamun's tomb are of solid gold or ivory. Others are as simple as wrapped balls of hair, which may be that of Tutankhamun and his wife. These were found within a small box, or casket.

Look at the ivory headrest, Catalogue number 48, and compare it with the small box, number 9, containing small balls of human hair wrapped in linen.

Decide which object would be more important for you to see, if you could choose only one. To help you decide, put a check in the chart below under the name of the object which, in your opinion, is better.

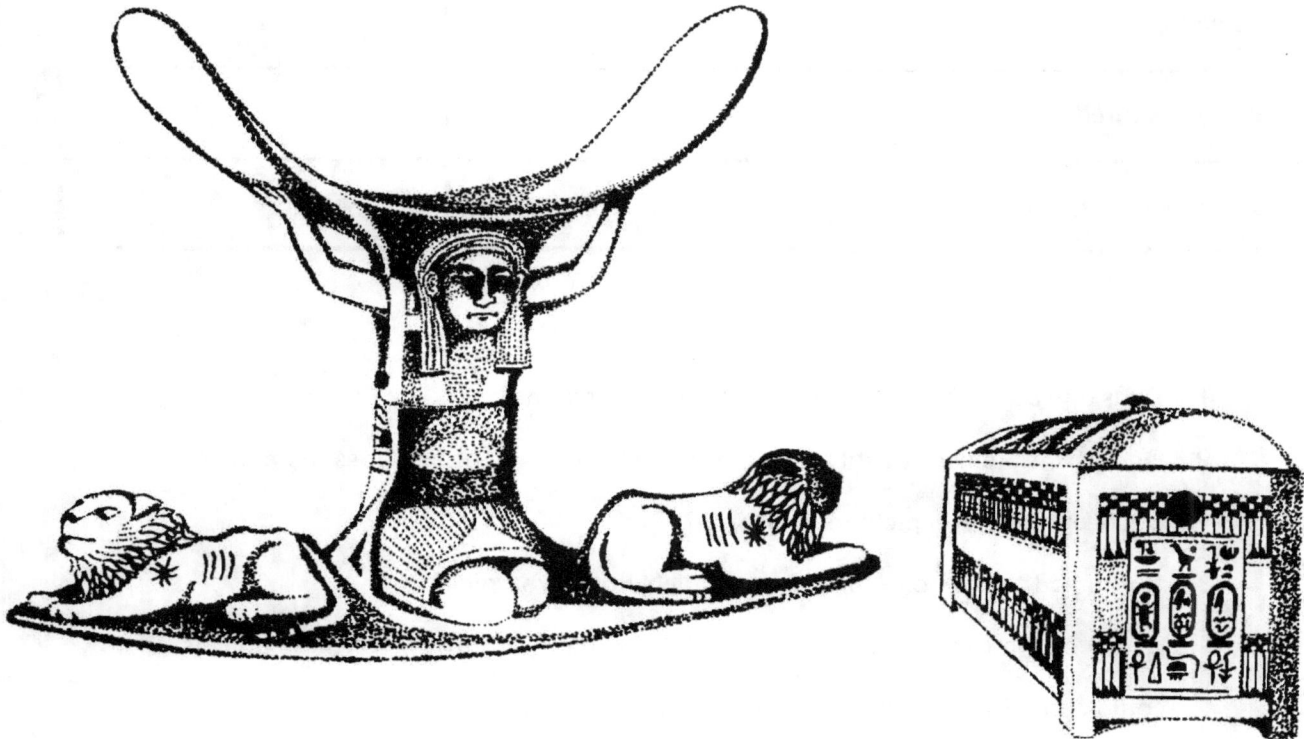

BASIS FOR DECISION	#48, HEADREST	#9, BOX WITH HAIR BALLS
Usefulness		
Neatness		
Craftsmanship		
Cost of materials		
Historical value		
Human interest		
Artistry required for production		
Value to royal family		

1. Does one object have more checks? If so, which one?

2. One of the items probably had more checks than the other. Does the number of checks help you pick your favorite?

3. If you had to pick only one to see, which would you pick?

4. Which do you think a museum would rather have, if only one of these objects could come for a display? Why did you reach this conclusion?

RATING YOUR EYE-Q

Most people have a clear mental picture when they imagine what a statue of an Egyptian pharaoh looks like. They can tell what the pharaoh will be wearing, whether he will be sitting or standing, and what he might be doing.

Imagine your mental picture of a typical Egyptian pharaoh. Using the questions on the next page to get you started, list as many details as you can. Work by yourself or in a small group.

Think about the following questions as you make your list.

1. Is he sitting or standing?

2. Is he wearing any decorations or jewelry?

3. Is he holding something in both hands?

4. Is his clothing plain or fancy?

5. Is he wearing anything on his feet?

6. Does he have anything covering his head?

7. Does he seem to be a real person?

8. Does he seem to be in motion?

9. Is his body symmetrical, that is, both sides shown to be exactly alike?

10. What is the primary color of the statue?

11. Does he have a beard?

1. _____

2. _____

3. _____

4. _____

5. _____

6. _____

7. _____

8. _____

9. _____

10. _____

11. _____

Now analyze your impressions and decide which are the three most common features of Egyptian statues of pharaohs. Write them in the spaces below:

Rule #1 _____

_____

Rule #2 _____

_____

Rule #3 _____

_____

To test your rules, look closely at four statues of King Tutankhamun shown on the next page; Catalogue numbers 17 and 41 show statues of him as a boy, and numbers 35 and 38 represent him as a man.

For each rule you predicted, give yourself a plus if the rule is proven to be true, a minus if not. Total your points.

Tutankhamun as a Boy

Tutankhamun as a Man

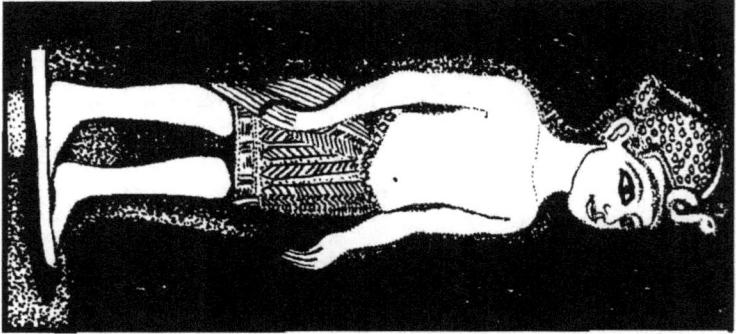

Rule #1 ___   ___   ___   ___

Rule #2 ___   ___   ___   ___

Rule #3 ___   ___   ___   ___

Total number of pluses   ___   ___   ___   ___

How did you do as an art expert? You can rate yourself using the following chart.

Score	Explanation
11-12	You are a genius in Egyptian art history. Maybe you should write a book.
9-10	The scarab brings you luck today. Your score brings you great respect.
7-8	No one would ever have guessed your wisdom! Great work.
5-6	Now, don't you feel a bit more humble? But don't feel bad. Check the facts below.
3-4	Tsk, tsk! Perhaps you should be a little more observant.
0-2	Miserable show! You are certainly missing the whole scene.

If your score was low, there is a good reason. Artists during the time of Tutankhamun were known to experiment with a variety of artistic styles. They were not predictable in their portrayal of the pharaoh, as previous artists had been.

Study this picture carefully. Using the clues on the next page, what do you see about the picture which breaks some rules of reality?

Look carefully at:

1. The hound

2. The bow case

3. The hands of the pharaoh

4. The reins of the horse

5. The plumes on the heads of the horses

6. The legs of the horses

7. The faces on the right side of the scene

Explanation: Egyptian art broke some rules of reality in order to keep objects from blocking other objects in a picture.

Pictures of King Tutankhamun, portraying him as an archer, are often equally surprising. Look at the illustration from Catalogue number 13, below, for an example.

Can you tell what is wrong with the picture below?

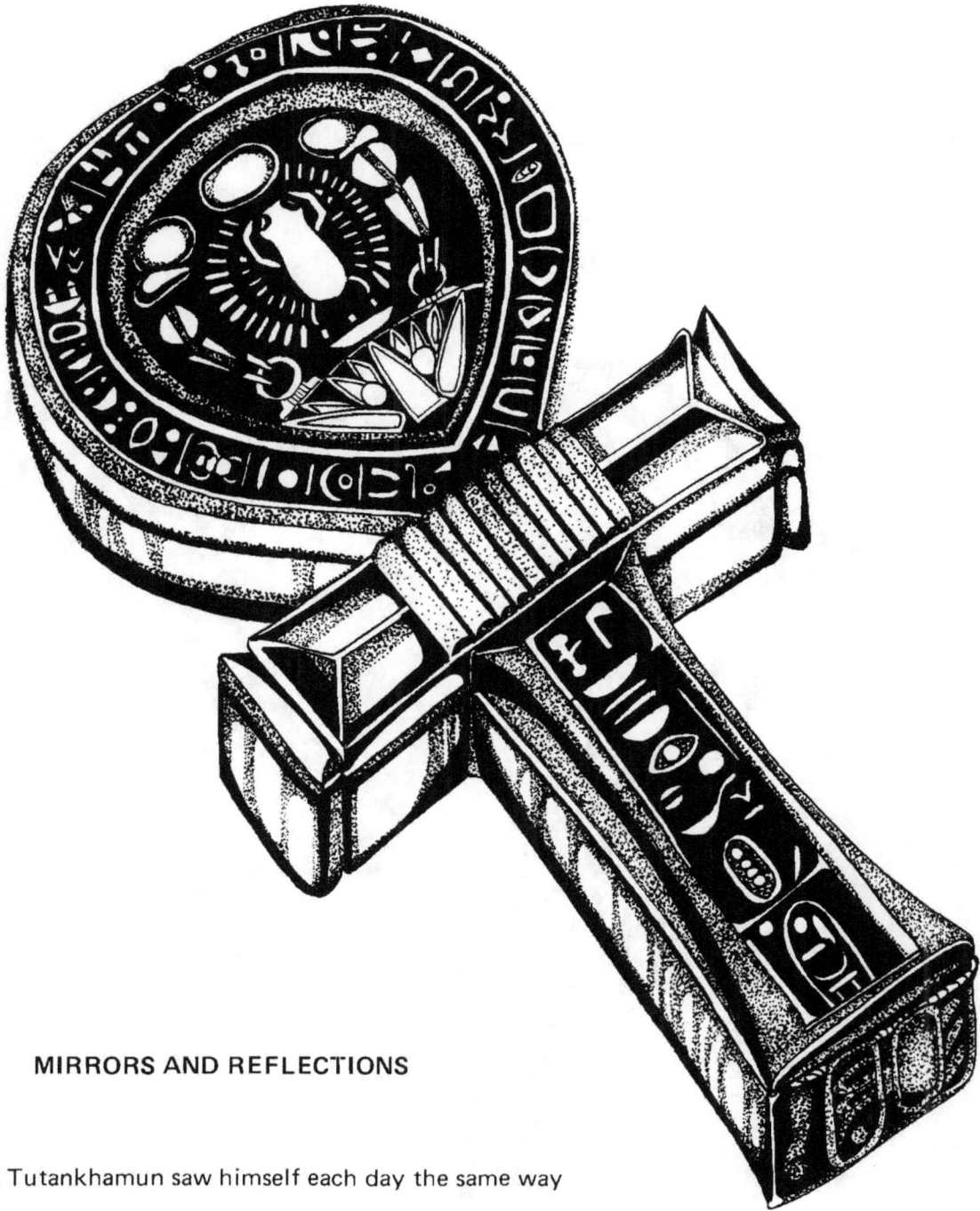

MIRRORS AND REFLECTIONS

King Tutankhamun saw himself each day the same way we do, as a reflection in a mirror. Look at Catalogue number 31, his mirror case. The metal mirror it contained has been stolen. The shape of the case forms the Egyptian hieroglyph for <u>ankh</u>, which means <u>mirror</u>, or <u>life.</u> This same word is found in the middle of Tut<u>ankh</u>amun's name.

Imagine you are looking into Tutankhamun's mirror. Try to draw a simple front view of yourself in it.

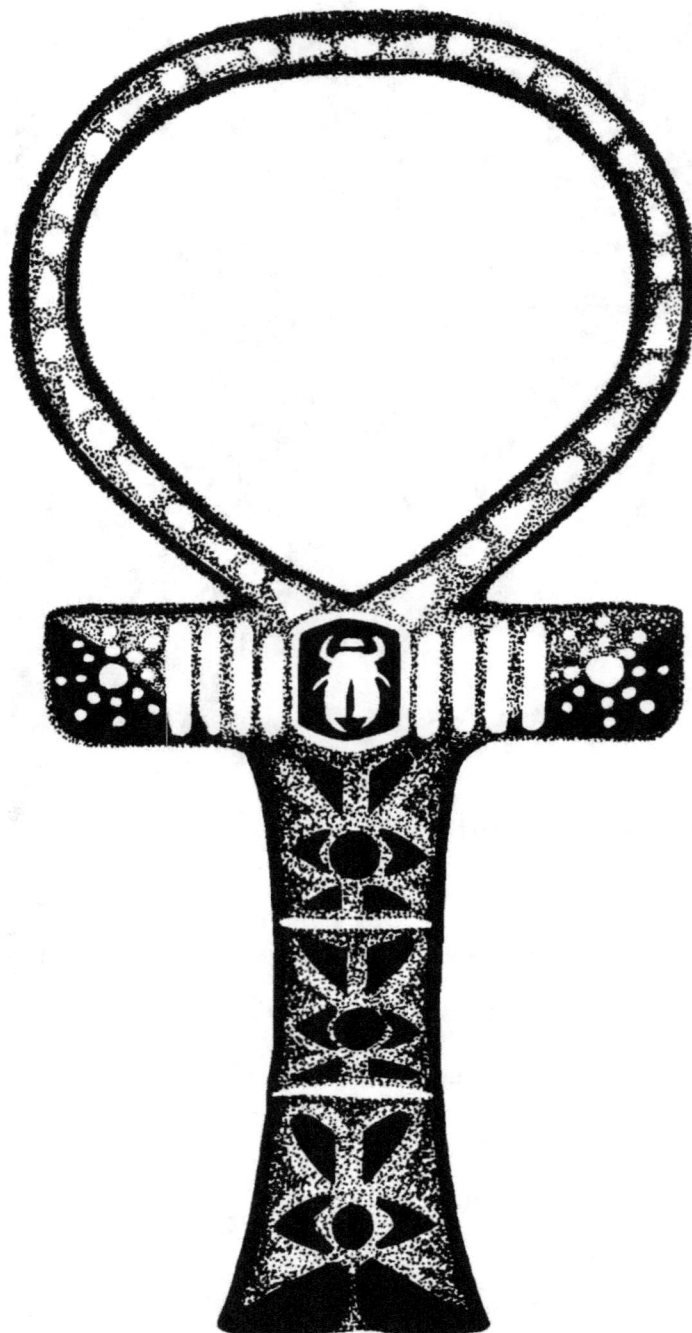

If you look into a mirror, you will see a full frontal view of your face. Rarely was King Tutankhamun shown in this way, unless he was shown in a three-dimensional form, like a sculpture or mask. For paintings on flat surfaces, side views were usually shown. Examples taken from Catalogue numbers 13 and 3 are illustrated below.

In a side view, an artist generally can show only half of a face. The artists who portrayed King Tutankhamun ignored reality and showed a view of the whole eye on the profile, or side view, of the face. With this method, the Egyptian artists combined the two directions for viewing a person, so that one could see front and side views at the same time.

An artist named Picasso also painted faces showing side and frontal views at the same time. He did so by adding the far side of the face to a profile of the drawing and keeping the same eye shape we saw in the paintings of King Tutankhamun. An example of one of Picasso's faces is seen below on the left.

Many people are fascinated by the faces of Picasso's subjects. On a full face portrait, he made a division into two areas, treating one as a profile with a full eye shape as we saw on the portrayals of King Tutankhamun.

Study the faces frame by frame, and you can see how he achieved two views at once:

The fourth frame is a space for you to try this technique for yourself.

A mirror reflects the way a person really looks. Artists can portray either a mirror-like image of a person or can break some rules of reality, as they did in some of the portrayals of King Tutankhamun.

You have already pictured yourself in a realistic, mirror image. You have also seen how the front and side views of a person's face can be combined into one image. Now try experimenting with some artistic techniques. The choices below will provide ways to do more than reflect a simple mirror image of your subject. Select one of the techniques and create a portrait in that way, either of yourself or of someone else.

1. Tear pieces of different colors of scrap paper to make a rough picture of your subject. All edges should be created by tearing, not cutting.

2. Try drawing a picture of a head, as seen from the back. A silhouette can be created by tracing the shadow of the subject's head as shown on a wall with the use of an opaque projector. Fill in the outline, showing hair, ears, neck, and collar. Or fill the outline with words and pictures.

3. Make a three-dimensional head, using a stuffed sock, a styrofoam ball, a wooden spoon, clay, a balloon, a bar of soap, or a box.

PUBLIC IMAGES — PRIVATE IMAGES

If you have ever worn a mask, you know how it feels to hide your real face and take on a different look. You know that your own face is unchanged, but you are presenting a new face to anyone looking at you. You can control what the other person can see, and the new image can bring you a sense of pleasure, of security, or of boldness.

Can you think of any situations in which a face mask might be used? What is the purpose(s) for each one?

Situations in which masks are used	Purpose(s) for the mask
1.	
2.	
3.	
4.	

Besides masking looks, people can also mask feelings to protect themselves from criticism or ridicule. Each person is known to others in some ways, and is hidden from others in some other ways. The known part might be called the public image of the person; the lesser-known part, the private imate. What aspects of yourself are known to others? What aspects of yourself are lesser known to others?

To explore and portray your public and private images, cut pictures and words that are reflections of yourself from magazines. You may also collect small objects that reflect your life values or memories. Put the "public you" images on the outside of a bag or box. Inside the container, put the pictures, words, and objects which portray more about the "private you." If you wish, when you are finished, you may close or tie up the container to keep the private images private.

Exchange and discuss your self-portrait with a partner. Then get into groups of four for further sharing:

1. What similarities did you find between your public image and that of others?

2. What additions would you like to make, after seeing what others did?

You may see something of King Tutankhamun as a public and private person by comparing three images of him shown in the following illustrations:

The gold mask (Catalogue number 25) showed the public image of Tutankhamun. It was placed directly over the linen wrappings of the mummy, to resemble the king's living image. This funeral mask showed King Tutankhamun in a formal, controlled, dignified pose, as people expected a pharaoh to look.

To view the king as he was portrayed in one of his private images, see the relief carving on the top of a small chest (Catalogue number 51) where he is shown as a young husband receiving flowers from his wife.

The scene shown on one side of the golden shrine (Catalogue number 13), shows the king and queen in another relaxed, informal pose.

Using some photographs of yourself, make two groups, one representing your public image in formal poses, and the other your private image in informal poses. Select the picture you like best of yourself in a formal pose and an informal pose.

Mount the two pictures carefully side by side. In a small group, share the pictures, and together, discuss these questions:

1. What things do you find are generally true of formal poses?

2. What things do you find are generally true of informal poses?

3. What things are similar between your informal poses and the informal scenes showing King Tutankhamun?

4. Do you prefer formal poses or informal poses of yourself? Why?

5. Why do you think formal poses are used to mark special events in a person's life?

ANIMALS AS SYMBOLS, THEN AND NOW

The names and pictures of animals are often used today to represent qualities which we like to associate with objects or people. To see how common this practice is, see how many animal names you can provide in the chart below:

Type of object/person described:	Animal names used:
1. cars	
2. symbols of our country	
3. sports teams	
4. symbols of peoples' religious beliefs	
5. clubs	

In addition, we have borrowed the names of many animals to make descriptive words about the way people act; sometimes the description is complimentary, sometimes not.

What animal names can you think of which have been borrowed to describe people?

Complimentary Words	Uncomplimentary Words

Now imagine you must choose one animal name or symbol for a new product in each situation listed:

1. You live in an area in which there will be a new professional football team. The team needs a name.

    Qualities suggested: _____

    Your team name: _____

2. You are the designer of a new line of cars and need a name to represent your product.

    Qualities suggested: _____

    Your car name: _____

3. You are a designer of a greeting card to be sold to people who are always late in sending their birthday greetings. Your card needs an animal picture to represent how you feel when you forget to mail things on time:

    Qualities suggested: _____

    Your animal symbol: _____

4. You own a big recreational resort development in the mountains. The resort needs a symbol on all of its advertising, and you would like to use an animal for that symbol.

    Qualities suggested: _____

    Your animal symbol: _____

During the reign of King Tutankhamun, the powers of animals were frequently linked with the power of the pharaoh. The pharaoh might also be helped by friendly gods symbolized by animals, or threatened by hostile gods in animal form. Before you see how some of the animal symbols were used on Tutankhamun's treasures, fill in the chart below, and on the next page.

Write in the name of the animal you think might be used in present-day symbolism. Then turn to the catalogue entries for the items indicated, and from the drawings or words found there, fill in the name of the animal shown on the treasures of King Tutankhamun.

CATEGORY	ANIMAL MOST LIKELY USED IN PRESENT-DAY SYMBOLISM	CATALOGUE NUMBER	ANIMAL ASSOCIATED WITH TREASURES OF KING TUTANKHAMUN
Animal symbol used to indicate a priest or god		4	
Animal associated with good luck		23, 37	
Animal motifs used as designs on household items		11, 12	
Animal used as symbol of government		16	
Animal whose feathers might be used for human comforts		18	

CATEGORY	ANIMAL MOST LIKELY USED IN PRESENT-DAY SYMBOLISM	CATALOGUE NUMBER	ANIMAL ASSOCIATED WITH TREASURES OF KING TUTANKHAMUN
Animal(s) you'd dread meeting in the water		35	
Animal shape often used in jewelry		32	
Animals which are extinct or very rare		4, 11	
Animal used to symbolize a great number of something		10	
Combination of two animals which when shown together, represent harmony between two traditional enemies		25	

Journey to a New Life

The year is 1870. You and your family have joined a group of pioneers who will travel from St. Louis, Missouri, to Oregon. Your covered wagon contains everything you can take to your new home, as well as things you will need on the journey. Other than food, clothing, and weapons, you will need to take along other items for the trip and for your new life out West. Write ten other items you would want to have along:

1. _____

2. _____

3. _____

4. _____

5. _____

6. _____

7. _____

8. _____

9. _____

10. _____

During the time of King Tutankhamun, it was believed that when pharaohs died, they took a journey to the afterlife. They would need the same things for this journey as they had needed and used in real life. Such necessities as food, clothing, and weapons were provided for them and placed in their tombs with their mummies.

Look at the categories in the chart below. First, fill in one or more items for each category that you think would be taken along on a trip in a prairie schooner. Using the Catalogue at the back, find an item, or items, used in the same way by King Tutankhamun in the afterlife.

Category	Pioneer in Prairie Schooner	King Tutankhamun in the Afterlife
Mode of travel		
Items of recreation		
Food and drink		
Family keepsakes (heirlooms)		
Defense		

Category	Pioneer in Prairie Schooner	King Tutankhamun in the Afterlife
Comforts		
Clothing and Jewelry		
Household furnishings		
Tools		
Utensils and storage containers		
Items for keeping personal records		
Religious items		
Pets or other animals		
Luxuries		
Items for making fire and light		

Now look back at the list of ten items on page 61. Did you fill in things on that list that later appeared in either column of the chart on the previous pages? If so, good thinking!

These two trips, that of a pioneer going out West, and that of a pharaoh journeying through the afterlife, were separated by over 3,000 years.

1. What did you find was similar about these two lists of items?

2. What did you find was different about the two lists?

3. Would you have added anything to either list? If so, what?

MAKING A LUNCH

You are going to make a lunch to eat a week from today. You must put your lunch in a box without a lid, or a glass jar without a top. After a week's time has passed, if you have planned carefully, you should be able to eat your lunch. List below the foods you plan to put in your lunch box.

Menu

ONE WEEK LATER ‒ ‒ ‒ ‒ ‒

Food Item	List of Ingredients:	How Does It Look?	Is There Any Sign of Deterioration?	How Much Longer Do You Think Each Item Would Have Lasted?

Did you pick something that contained preservatives?	Did you pack any foods that were dehydrated?	What did you learn about the life expectancy of food products?
What foods would you have used if you could have used a covered container?	What things can you think of that can destroy or ruin food?	What processes are used to preserve and protect foods?

PREPARING A POMANDER

(Mummifying an Apple)

The process of mummifying is partly a drying process, employing chemicals and spices to aid in preserving a plant or animal. Time is needed to do the drying and treating. You can observe the stages of this process by using chemicals and spices to dry an apple. While different spices and more time were employed in the mummification of King Tutankhamun, the process of mummification is basically what you will be doing when you prepare a pomander, using a small apple. A small lemon, lime, or orange may also be used, although the process may take four weeks instead of one.

MATERIALS: Small apple

2 — 3 boxes of whole cloves

½ — 1 teaspoon ground cinnamon

½ — 1 teaspoon orrisroot if citrus is used (orrisroot may be obtained from the drugstore)

1 brown bag or plastic bag

PROCESS: 1. Wash and dry the apple.

2. Push cloves into the apple, using a cuticle stick to start holes if the skin is tight. Be careful to cover the apple evenly, without crowding the cloves, since the fruit will eventually shrink.

3. Set the apple in a bag and add the cinnamon. Shake thoroughly. If citrus fruit is used, shake with equal amounts of cinnamon and orrisroot.

4. Wrap the apple loosely in a square of cloth, or place it on a dish or foil-covered box top, so that it won't roll.

5. Store in a dry place for at least a week. If a citrus is used, you may need up to a month for the drying to be completed.

6. When the fruit is dry, you may wrap it in a square of decorative netting and tie it with ribbon or yarn. You can then hang the pomander in a closet, or place it in a drawer or chest to freshen the air.

If you wish to observe the process of the drying as it occurs, make several pomanders, and cut one in half each time you wish to check. You can use this comparison chart to record your findings, from the beginning of the experiment to the end:

Ways to Compare	Typical Condition of Your Apple/Citrus	Checkpoint #1 _____ Days	Checkpoint #2 _____ Days	Checkpoint #3 _____ Days
Color				
Moisture Content				
Aroma				
Size				
Texture				
Weight				

The mummification process, to prepare the body of King Tutankhamun for its journey to the after-life, took 70 days. Most internal vital organs, other than the heart, were removed and put into tightly sealed containers called canopic jars. The body was dried with salt and other chemicals before it was ready for wrapping. One hundred forty-three objects were contained among the many layers of linen cloth strips surrounding the mummy. The objects wrapped next to the body of King Tutankhamun were believed to serve as charms, or amulets, and were located over the parts of the body they were meant to protect. To discover some of these objects hidden in the linen bandages, look in the Catalogue at the items indicated below. Fill in the information on the chart:

Catalogue Number	Type of Object	How Many Placed on the Body
20		2 (one of iron, one of gold)
21		13 (seven on right and six on left)
22		2
23, 24		17
25		1 (placed on top of the bandages)

PRESERVING HISTORY ON PAPER

After preparing something to last a long time, a person must be able to keep moisture out. If an absorbent material is not kept dry, it may deteriorate quickly. The challenge of the next activity is to find a way to preserve a collection of postage stamps.

DIRECTIONS: Select five postage stamps, new or used, that you think would show something worth noticing or remembering about the present historical era. Choose one of the methods described on the following page to mount or display these stamps so that they cannot be ruined by moisture, light, or air.

Suggested Methods

Cover them with layers of the following:

Wax   1. Arrange stamps on an index card.

           2. Iron this display between two pieces of waxed paper larger than the card.

           3. Trim the waxed paper edges neatly, leaving a margin of at least one inch all the way around.

Plastic 1. Arrange stamps on an index card.

           2. Wrap one layer of clear plastic, such as a vegetable bag from the supermarket, over and under the display.

           3. Place one sheet of newspaper over the plastic so that no plastic shows.

           4. Iron over the newspaper around the edges of the card so that the plastic edges melt and stick together, forming a seal for the card.

White Glue   1. Arrange stamps on an index card.

2. Mix in a small container, or on a piece of aluminum foil, one tablespoon white glue and one tablespoon water. Mix well. Apply it over the stamps and card with fingers, brush, or sponge.

3. Let it dry thoroughly (10 — 15 minutes).

4. Apply two more layers of the white glue and water mixture, allowing the card to dry thoroughly between applications.

Nail Polish   1. Arrange stamps on an index card.

2. Cover the card with a layer of clear nail polish.

3. Let it dry thoroughly (at least half an hour).

4. Apply two more layers of nail polish, allowing the card to dry thoroughly between applications.

Salt   1. Find a spice jar or baby food jar with a lid.

2. Fill the jar with alternating layers of salt and a stamp.

3. Screw the top on the jar tightly.

Tape   1. Place stamps on an index card.

2. Cover the card with strips of cellophane tape.

Compare methods by discussing the following questions:

1.   Method most commonly used:

2.   Reasons for choosing that method:

3.   Method least used:

4.   Reasons for not choosing that method:

5.   Method which will probably work the best:

6.   Reasons for choosing that method:

You may wish to place your finished projects outside in a safe place or bury them. Leave them for at least two weeks, or longer, and then examine them. Observe what changes, if any, have taken place. Then decide which method was least destructive to the stamps. Which was most destructive?

HISTORICAL ASIDE:

There was no paper product found in the 5,000 items taken from King Tutankhamun's tomb:

— Why do you think paper products were not placed in the tomb?

— Which, if any, of the methods you used were unavailable to the Egyptians?

FOLLOW-UP:

If your stamp display were to survive for 3,000 years, what guesses might the people living at that time make about you and your culture from the following:

1. The pictures and writing on the stamps?

2. The materials used in preservation of the display?

WRAPPING AN ARTIFACT

The process of wrapping a mummy took a great deal of patience and care. The linen wrapping not only covered the body, but held objects in place over parts of the body they were meant to protect.

Placed in the tomb around the mummy were many objects which would be of value to the person in the afterlife. By examining those objects, much can be learned about that period of history.

If a person from some future time could open a time capsule in which we had placed objects we considered of value, certain things would be revealed about us and our way of life.

Your next project will be to make such a time capsule to exchange with another person or group. The challenge will be to choose the objects which reveal the most about our values and our way of life.

PROCEDURE:

1. Think of a list of objects which tell a lot about our culture. Consider their usefulness, beauty, the materials from which they are made, or some other criteria.

2. Collect ten of these objects or find a picture of ten to tell about the time in which we live.

3. Choose one of the ten objects you think tells the most about our culture.

4. Wrap strips of newspaper or rags around the object considered to be the most important.

5. Continue layering, including each of the other nine objects somewhere in the wrappings.

6. Exchange your time capsule with that created by another group and unwind it carefully. List the objects you find inside.

7. Analyze the objects selected by the other group. For each object included, determine what information could be revealed about our values and our way of life.

8. Compare the item placed in the center of their time capsule with the item you placed there. From which object could you learn the most?

LOOKING BACK

Which object, of the fifty-five on display, do you think is:

The strangest? _____

The most beautiful? _____

The most useful? _____

The most unlike anything
    we have today? _____

The most valuable? _____

The one that made Tutankhamun
    seem most human? _____

The heaviest? _____

The most comfortable? _____

The one you liked best which
    showed an animal? _____

Now that you know much more than you once did about the treasures from the tomb of King Tutankhamun, pick out your favorite five. To refresh your memory, refer to the list of objects on pages 23 and 24, or to the Catalogue.

1. _____

2. _____

3. _____

4. _____

5. _____

Answer these questions:

1. Were any of the five objects listed among those you considered in the semi-finals of the Treasures Tournament, page 28?

2. Was your nomination for purchase in that lesson among your five favorites?

3. Were any of your five favorites in the list you made above?

Compare your list with someone else and see if you chose any of the same objects for your favorite five.

1. PAINTED WOODEN HEAD OF KING
   TUTANKHAMUN AS A BABY

   He is shown at the moment of birth emerg-
   ing from a lotus blossom, and symbolizing
   the sun god.

2. WHITE ALABASTER CUP

   These cups were shaped like lotus blooms.
   Present evidence suggests the white lotus
   cups were used for drinking, while the blue
   lotus cups were used for ritualistic purposes.

3. TRUMPET AND WOODEN STOPPER

   Made of bronze or copper with gold overlay,
   this one of only three instruments preserved
   from ancient Egypt. A wooden stopper
   fitting into the tube and bell was found with
   the trumpet. The stopper was used with a
   cloth as a cleaning instrument or to pre-
   vent damage when the trumpet was not in
   use. The exact sound heard by the ancient
   people has recently been reproduced using
   this very trumpet. Figures on the bell suggest it was used for military purposes.

4. CARVED LEOPARD'S HEAD

Part of a real leopard skin cape, this head was worn by the priest during a ceremony called "Opening of the Mouth." The purpose of this ceremony was to restore life to the mummified body.

5. CROOK AND FLAIL (ROD AND STAFF)

These were carried by pharaohs during ceremonial occasions. This flail is probably the one King Tutankhamun held as a nine-year-old boy at his coronation. The king's name in its early form, Tutankhaton, and his throne name, Nebkheperura, were found written on the base of the flail handle.

6. BELT BUCKLE

Made of gold, this shows King Tutankhamun as a warrior returning from battle, even though it is unlikely he ever actually took part in any warfare. Captives shown in front of the chariot are from Asia and Nubia. Because Asia lay to the northeast and Nubia to the south, this would have been an impossibility for any one-war campaign.

7. PORTABLE CHEST

Made of ebony and some type of red wood, possibly cedar, this chest is an example of the exquisite use of materials by Egyptian craftsmen. Poles used to carry the chest could be completely concealed. It is the only known example of an ancient Egyptian portable chest.

8. CHILD'S CHAIR

This chair was probably used by Tutankhamun, as a child. The wood may be ebony from Africa, and is inlaid with ivory.

9. MINIATURE ALABASTER CASKET

This held many items including two balls of hair wrapped in linen, probably from the heads of King Tutankhamun and his wife Ankhesenamun, and thought to have been symbolizing some kind of contract.

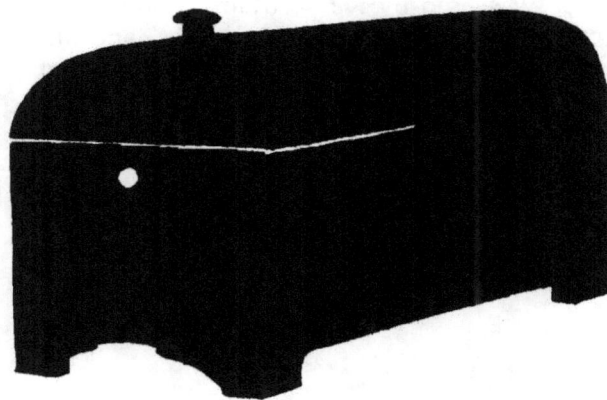

10. WHITE ALABASTER VASE FOR OILS

About fifty of these were found in the tomb; they were used to store precious perfumed oils. At either end of a design representing a papyrus swamp, shown on the level of the base of the vase, is a figure of a tadpole mounted on a ring of rope. The tadpole was the hieroglyphic sign meaning 100,000, and the rope, infinity. When combined with the sign for life, the significance was a wish for life lasting 100,000 times infinity.

11. FOLDING STOOL

The stool has a reverse leopard skin pattern, buff markings on a black background, on the seat, and a carved leopard tail hanging down one end.

12. CHAIR FROM CORONATION

It is likely that this chair, with its lion paw legs, was used by King Tutankhamun at his coronation. The elegant carvings and inscriptions emphasize the fact that the king was of divine origin and had descended from the gods.

13. GOLD-PLATED SHRINE, OR CASE FOR A GODDESS

The outside is decorated with scenes showing King Tutankhamun and his wife in many poses depicting their life, as well as cartouches and birds. On the pedestal found inside can be seen the imprint of the feet of a statuette, probably of the queen, which had been stolen.

14. ALABASTER LAMP RESEMBLING THREE LOTUS BLOSSOMS

This lamp was carved from a single piece of alabaster. It shows the flowers on a lotus plant, growing from the bed of a pond. When it was found, traces of oil were still inside.

15. CARVING OF A HEADLESS ANIMAL, HUNG FROM A POLE

This carving represented Anubis, the god of embalming. By its placement in the burial chamber and the inscriptions on the base, it was likely meant for King Tutankhamun's use in the afterlife.

16. JAR FOR OILS, WITH RESTING LION ON LID

The lion on the lid was probably intended to represent the image of the king, suggesting his lion-like character.

17. SMALL GOLD STAFF

A small gold figure of King Tutankhamun stand on a platform attached to a tube-like staff. Its exact use is unknown, but some evidence suggests he may have used this at the time of his coronation.

18. OSTRICH-FEATHER FAN

The ends of the 15 white and 15 brown ostrich feathers used for the plumes of this fan may still be seen in the holes where they were once attached. There is an inscription on the long wooden pole forming the handle, and the scenes on both sides of the palm show King Tutankhamun hunting the ostriches and bringing home their feathers.

19. LIDDED CASE FOR OILS, WITH DOUBLE CARTOUCHE DESIGN

The boxes had small figures of King Tutankhamun on the back and front. In one cartouche, the king is shown with a black face, perhaps associated with the black soil of the Nile, source of plant life. Thus, the color black was associated with the wish for new life for the king.

20. GOLDEN DAGGER AND SHEATH

Vivid animal designs which decorate the sheath, and the ornate designs on the shaft, are excellent examples of the goldsmith's artistry and skill. It is likely that only royalty owned daggers of gold.

21. BEAD BRACELET

From the right arm of the mummy of King Tutankhamun, this shows an **udjat** eye, which was a human eye and eyebrow with the markings of a falcon's head. This charm, popular in ancient Egypt, was used to ward off sickness or restore life to the dead.

22. GOLD RINGS

Two rings were found wrapped with the mummy of King Tutankhamun. The pictures show important Egyptian gods.

85

23. FLEXIBLE COLLAR IN THE FORM OF A VULTURE

This collar, with counterweight, was found wrapped with the mummy. It covered the whole chest and was thought to provide magical protection. These were used only on the dead, and were very different from the bead or gold collars worn in life.

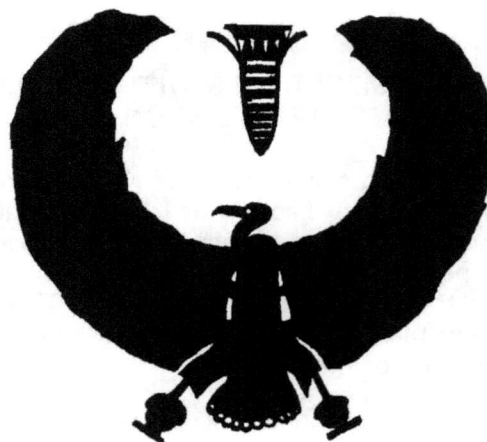

24. NECKLACE WITH VULTURE PENDANT

This was found on the king's neck in the 11th or 12th layer of linen bandages, close to the mummy. The fact that it was so close to his body indicated this was a personal possession he had worn during his lifetime.

25. GOLD MASK FOUND OVER THE HEAD AND SHOULDERS OF THE MUMMY

This solid gold mask is thought to be an exact likeness of the king. It is probably the most famous work of art from Tutankhamun's tomb. On the forehead is shown the outlines of two animals, the vulture and the cobra. The vulture symbolized King Tutankhamun's power over upper Egypt, and the cobra, over lower Egypt.

26. GOLD PECTORAL WITH EMBLEMS OF THE SUN AND MOON (Ornament worn over the chest)

This necklace is inlaid with lapis lazuli and colored glass. The two symbols which are used to represent the sun god, the scarab beetle and the falcon, are combined in this pectoral. The scarab serves as the body of a falcon with outstretched wings.

27. FALCON PECTORAL

Holding in its talons the signs for life and infinity, the falcon represents the god of the sun.

28. CARTOUCHE-SHAPED BOX

In Egypt, the cartouche contained the name and description of a pharaoh. Originally, this oval shape was formed by a loop of rope with the ends tied together, and the Egyptians called it a **shen**, meaning to encircle. Thus we see the underlying idea of the king as ruler of all that the sun encircled.

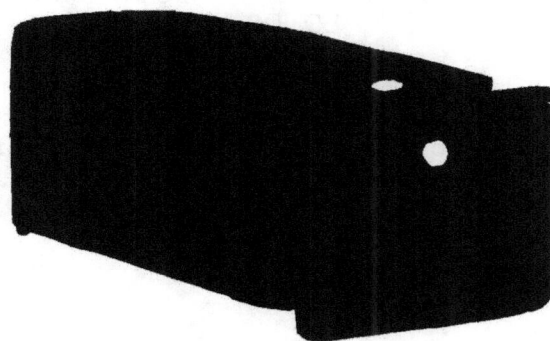

29. GOLD EARRINGS

Made in the shape of birds with the heads of ducks and the wings of falcons, these pieces of jewelry were among the few things found in the cartouche-shaped wooden box (Catalogue number 28). Although King Tutankhamun probably wore these earrings as a boy, he may have discontinued their use as he grew older. This may have been the reason the earrings were in a box, rather than on the mummy.

30. MIRROR CASE

The design is in the shape of the hieroglyphic sign **ankh**, which means life.

31. NECKLACE WITH MOON EMBLEM AND LOTUS COUNTERPOISE

The front side of this necklace shows the journey of the moon across the sky. The gold counterweight is decorated with papyrus and lotus designs.

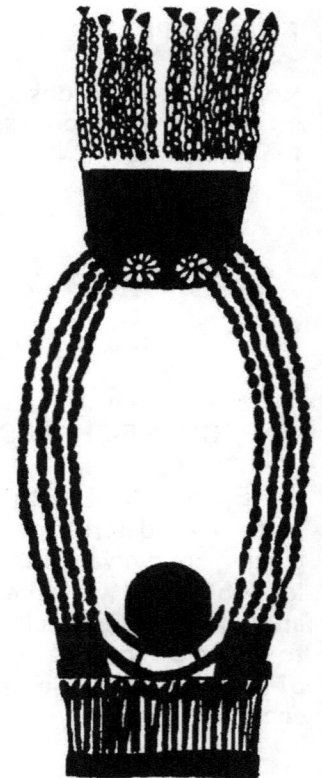

32. SCARAB BEETLE BRACELET

This piece of jewelry is decorated with a scarab beetle encrusted with lapis lazuli. It was found in the cartouche-shaped box (Catalogue number 28).

33. PEN HOLDER

This carved wooden tube was meant to be used for holding Tutankhamun's pen in the afterlife. It is not believed that he did any writing during his lifetime.

34. PAPYRUS BURNISHER: PAPER POL-ISHER

This ivory and gold tool was used by scribes to polish sheets of papyrus to make them smooth. Papyrus was used like paper.

35. STATUE OF KING TUTANKHAMUN WITH HARPOON

This golden statue shows the King preparing to harpoon a hippopotamus from a boat. The hippopotamus represented Seth, the god of evil. Sometimes Seth was represented as a crocodile. This statue represents Tutankhamun performing a religious rite, rather than participating in a real hunt.

36. MODEL BOAT

This may have been intended for King Tutankhamun's use in the afterlife, for his journeys to sacred places, or it may have been a model of a boat that was used to carry mourners to his funeral.

37. GOLDEN STATUE REPRESENTING A COBRA AS A GOD

The wooden cobra, with gold overlay, represented a god who would help guard King Tutankhamun on his journey through the underworld.

38. STATUE OF TUTANKHAMUN RIDING ON A LEOPARD

There is some evidence the black-colored leopards were connected with the king's journey through the dark underworld. The king was associated with the sun god and was, therefore, golden in color.

39. STATUE OF A GOD, PTAH

The gilded statue of the god, Ptah was associated with the seat of government and the capitol city of Memphis, in Egypt. It was believed by some that Ptah created the world, the other gods, people and all animals.

40. CARVED MUMMY OF KING TUTANKHA- MUM LYING IN STATE

The miniature statue of the king is lying on a funerary bed shaped like two lions. The bird and falcon lying beside the body represent two of the forms the king may have taken when he chose to revisit his mummified body.

41. SQUATTING SOLID GOLD FIGURE OF A KING

This figure was intended to be worn as a necklace. It is not typical of poses of Egyptian kings, because the king is squatting rather than seated or standing. It may have represented an earlier king, Ahmenhotpe III, but the pierced ears tended to suggest it was an image of Tutankhamun, in whose time pierced ears were fashionable for young men.

42. WOODEN CARVING OF TUTANKHAMUN

One of 413 such **shawabty** figures found in his tomb, these served as substitutes for the king when the god Osiris demanded that he perform manual labor.

43. WOODEN FIGURE OF THE GODDESS SELKET, OVERLAID WITH GOLD

This golden statue is one of four goddesses guarding the chest containing the mummified internal organs of King Tutankhamun. Selket's emblem, a scorpion, is placed on her head. The fact that her head is turned to the left broke with the traditional Egyptian style of art.

44. ALABASTER STOPPER FOR CANOPIC CHEST, RESEMBLING HEAD OF TUT-ANKHAMUN

This is one of the four stoppers used with the chest that held the gold miniature coffins that contained King Tutankhamun's mummified internal organs.

45. MINIATURE COFFIN FOR ONE OF THE KING'S INTERNAL ORGANS

Four miniature coffins, made of gold and each of which contained one of King Tutankhamun's mummified internal organs, were placed inside the alabaster chest (Catalogue number 44).

46. DOUBLE-SIDED GAME BOARD

This is the largest of four gaming boards found in the tomb. Evidence indicated this was a favorite pastime of King Tutankhamun. While the exact rules of the games are not known, the games resembled two commonly played in Egypt.

47. FLASK OF ALABASTER

A finely carved alabaster flask, or bottle-shaped container, this illustrates the revival of an outstanding achievement by Egyptian craftsmen: carving containers from stone.

48. HEADREST

Made of ivory, this was of a design never before found in ancient Egyptian art. The curved support represents the sky, and the lions, the earth.

49. MODEL OF A FOLDING STOOL

Painted with gilded decorations, this model was probably made of acacia wood, one of the few Egyptian woods suitable for furniture. The decorative hieroglyphic sign represents the union of northern and southern Egypt.

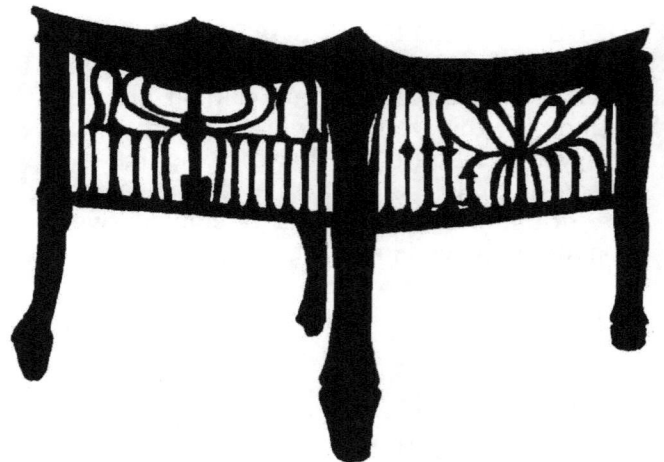

50. VASE SHAPED LIKE A POMEGRANATE

This vase was made of either silver or electrum (an alloy of gold and silver) and was decorated with carvings of cornflowers and leaves. The pomegranate, brought from western Asia, was uncommon enough during the time of Tutankhamun to attract special interest in ancient Egypt.

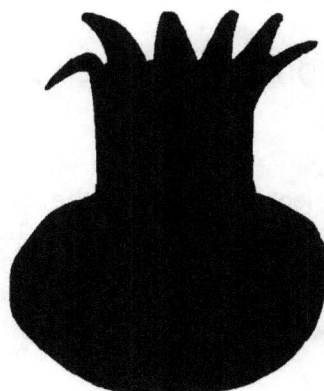

51. WOODEN CLOTHING CHEST WITH CARVINGS OF THE KING AND QUEEN

This elaborately carved and inlaid box shows one of only four pictures found in the tomb of King Tutankhamun and his queen together. It is likely the chest once held some of the king's ceremonial robes.

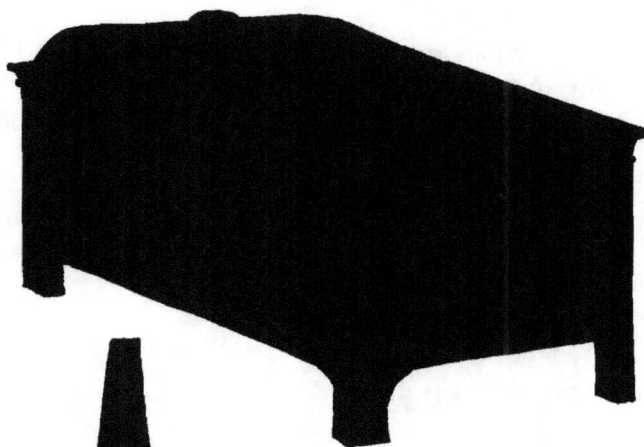

52. ROYAL SCEPTER WITH ELABORATE GOLD DESIGNS

Scepters like this, showing animal sacrifices, were often held by the person who presented offerings during temple rituals or funeral services.

53. JAR FOR OILS, SHAPED LIKE STAND-
ING LION

A hollow alabaster jar for storing precious
oils, this object is carved in the shape of a
lion standing on its hind legs. The lion form
was likely chosen because of its connection
with the god, Bes, a diety associated with
pleasure.

54. JAR FOR OILS, RESEMBLING RESTING
IBEX, OR DEER

In this carving, real ibex horns were used;
the missing horn was most likely stolen by
ancient robbers, trying to get to the oils
inside.

55. DECORATED BOW

One of the most elaborate bows among the
fifty weapons discovered in the tomb,
this type was introduced into Egypt by
Asian immigrants.

ANSWERS TO THE TWENTY QUESTIONS

ON THE GUESSING PAGE

1. False   King Tutankhamun was not buried beneath a pyramid.

2. False   His tomb contained over 5,000 objects.

3. False   He ruled from about age 9 to 18.

4. True   These weights were called counterpoises.

5. False   No scrolls or paper products were found in the tomb.

6. True   There were four game boards found in the tomb. Boomerangs had been in use in Egypt for at least five centuries before the time of King Tutankhamun.

7. False   Too many preserving oils were used in preparing his mummy. The only parts of the mummy that were well-preserved were under the gold mask and the golden toe and finger guards. The rest of the mummy was actually burned from too many oils.

8. True   The **London Times** and many ministers led the debate over whether or not archeologists had the right to disturb a burial place.

9. False   Moisture that had seeped in had turned leather items to a sticky, melted mass.

10. False   Queen Ankhesenamun was alive when King Tutankhamun was buried. She is represented in the tomb in drawings.

11. True   Precious oils were considered even more valuable than gold.

12. False   The boat was merely a model. Only the suggestion of a boat was needed.

13. False   The bodies of all people, as well as animals, were embalmed to insure their continued existence in an afterlife.

14. False   The mummification process took 70 days.

15. False   It was believed that King Tutankhamun became the god Anubis, who took the form of a dog, during one stage of his transformation in the afterlife.

16. False   Over the tomb entrance Howard Carter found the remains of workers' huts that had been erected during the building of the tomb of Ramasses VI.

17. True   He waited the time it took for Lord Carnarvon, who was financing the search for the tomb, to travel from England to be present for the opening.

18. False   Carter had been searching for the tomb of King Tutankhamun for years.

19. False   Unlike gold, silver was very rare in ancient Egypt. Very few silver items were found in the tomb.

20. False   Many layers of linen bandages were found wrapped around the body, enough to hide 143 objects, such as jewelry and good luck charms.